CREATURES FROM THE DARKEST DEPTHS OF THE SEA

Ocean Animals Book
Children's Marine Life Books

BABY PROFESSOR

EDUCATION KIDS

Speedy Publishing LLC

40 E. Main St. #1156

Newark, DE 19711

www.speedypublishing.com

Copyright 2017

Let's look at some of the creatures who share this Earth with us, but live in places where we can't live. We may never see these creatures outside of books—and we might never want to meet some of them in real life!

THE DEEP OCEAN

Humans live mostly on the land. We make use of the sea, for traveling and fishing, but we normally stay at or near the top of the oceans.

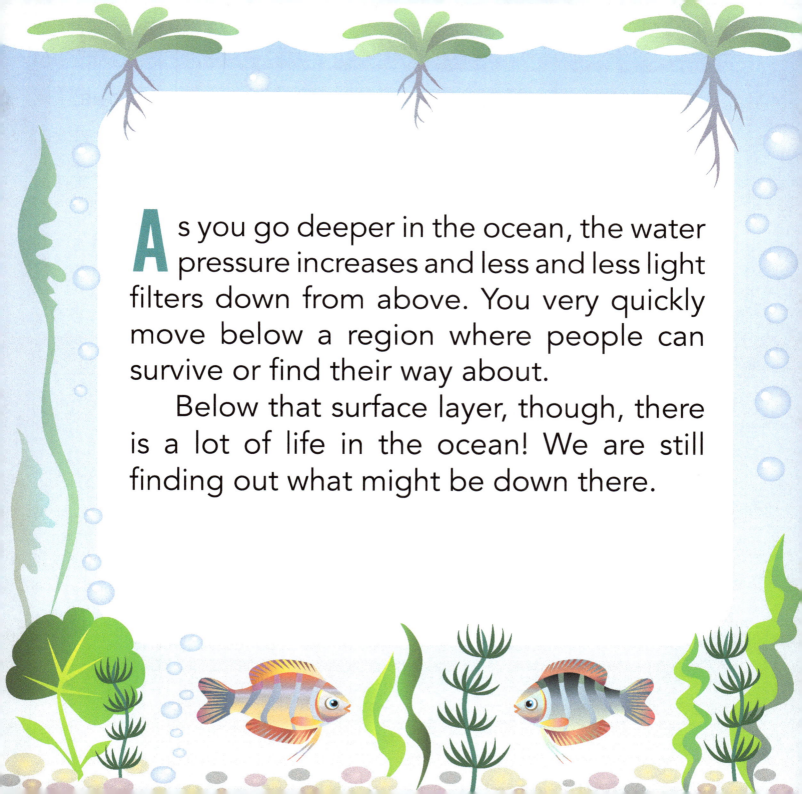

As you go deeper in the ocean, the water pressure increases and less and less light filters down from above. You very quickly move below a region where people can survive or find their way about.

Below that surface layer, though, there is a lot of life in the ocean! We are still finding out what might be down there.

A lot of these creatures look weird and monstrous, but really few are dangerous to humans. What is dangerous to us is where they live: the water pressure at the bottom of the ocean is so powerful it would flatten you like a pancake in no time. It's amazing these creatures can survive at all!

DRAGONFISH

FISH OF THE DEEP

DRAGONFISH

Dragonfish spend most of their lives almost two kilometers deep in the ocean. But dragonfish eggs can be found on the surface because they are light enough to float. Like many deep-sea fish, the dragonfish can use "bioluminescence" to create its own light. It has a lure on its lower jaw that it can light up to attract littler fish, which the dragonfish can then attack.

STARGAZER

The stargazer hides in the sand deep in the ocean and then projects itself upward to attack a fish that passes close by above it. To help it live this life, the stargazer has both its eyes and its mouth on the top of its head!

Some stargazers can also deliver an electric charge to stun the animal they are attacking.

STARGAZER

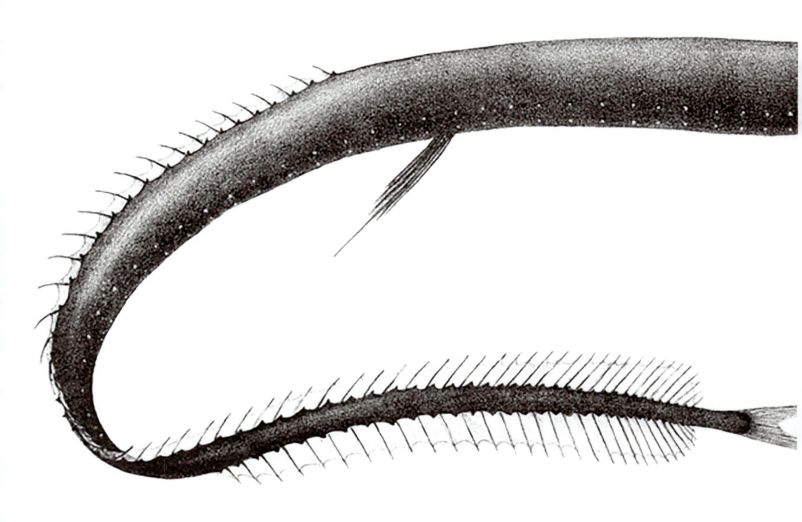

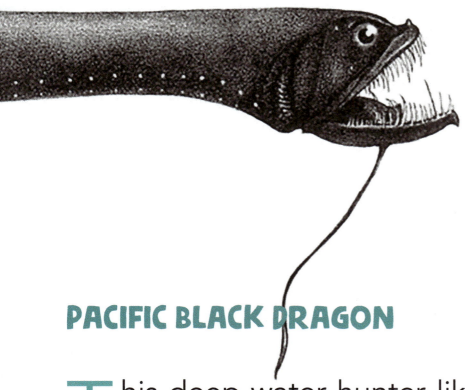

PACIFIC BLACK DRAGON

This deep-water hunter likes to eat fish that glow with bioluminescence. To be able to sneak up on such fish, the black dragon has a stomach that blocks the light of its previous meals from glowing through.

ANGLERFISH

The anglerfish has what looks like a fishing line with a lure extending from the top of its head. When a small fish comes close to see if the lure is food, the anglerfish strikes!

HATCHETFISH

HATCHETFISH

The deep-water hatchetfish gets its name from the shape of its body. It has tube-shaped eyes that look up from the depths toward the surface, so the fish can see and catch food that is sinking down from shallower water.

BARRELEYE

The barreleye, or "spook fish", is like the hatchetfish in that it has two eyes that face upward to see falling things it may want to eat. The name of the fish comes from the distinctive transparent dome that covers the eyes.

VIPERFISH

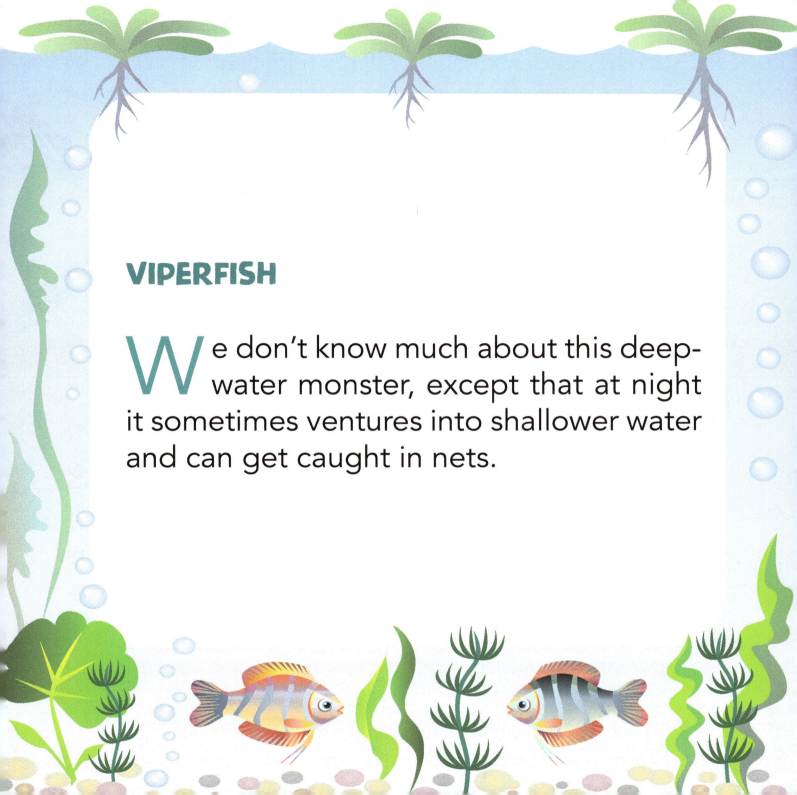

VIPERFISH

We don't know much about this deep-water monster, except that at night it sometimes ventures into shallower water and can get caught in nets.

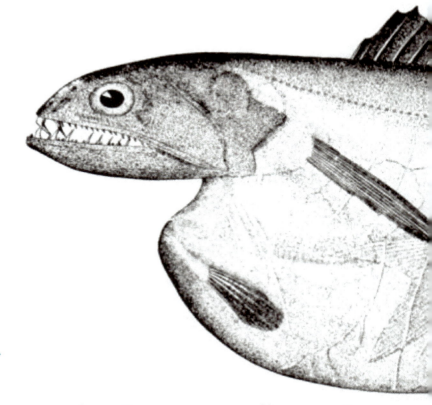

BLACK SWALLOWER

This fish is also known as the "great swallower". It can open its mouth wide enough to take in other fish that are as much as ten times as large as it is!

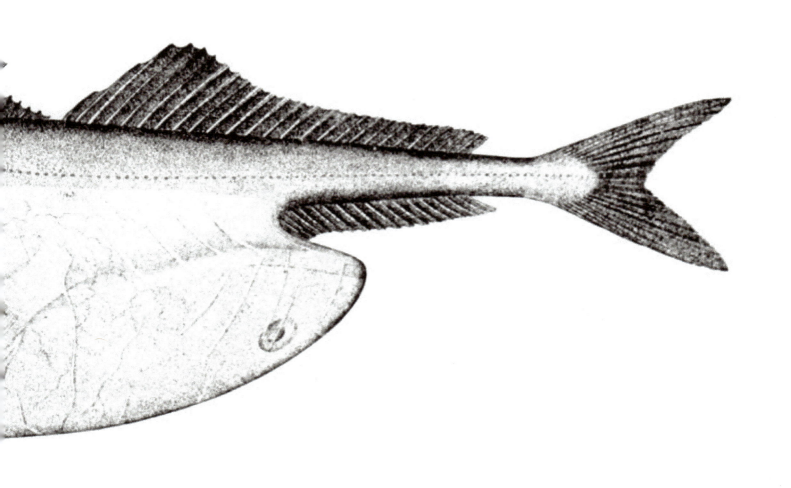

BLACK SWALLOWER

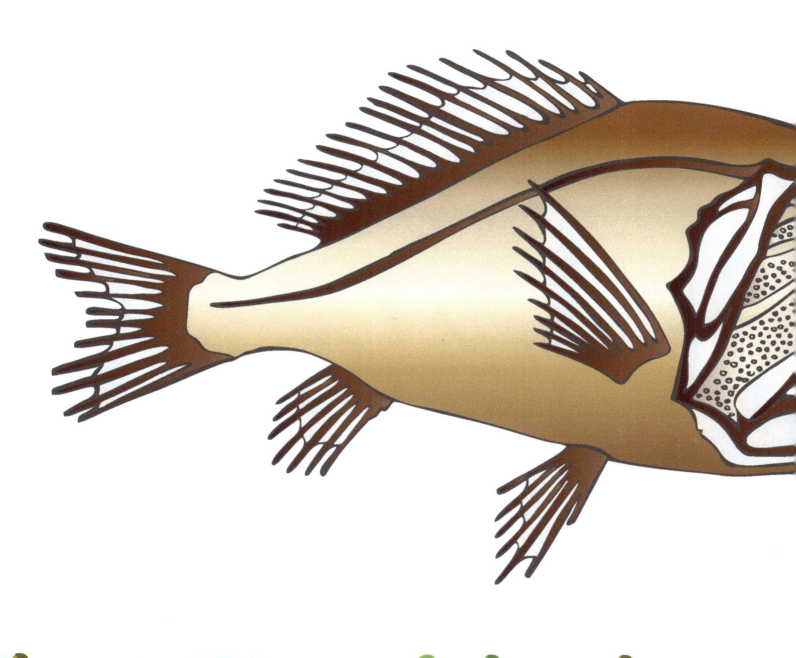

FANGTOOTH

FANGTOOTH

The fangtooth sounds and looks scary, but it is no threat to you. One reason is that it is very small. The other is that it lives as deep as 5,000 meters—if we visited there the sea pressure would crush us, so the little fangtooth would be the least of our problems.

The fish may be small, but it has larger teeth compared to its body size than any other fish we know of.

COFFINFISH

The coffinfish looks like a balloon covered in spikes. The spikes help defend the fish against others that might want to eat it, but it can also puff itself up to many times its normal size. This frightens most predators away.

The coffinfish has a lure on its head that it dangles ahead of it to attract tasty fish close enough that the coffinfish can attack them.

COFFINFISH

FRILLED SHARK

SHARKS

FRILLED SHARK

The frilled shark lives deep in the Atlantic and Pacific oceans. As far as we can tell, it is as it was millions of years ago, a sort of swimming fossil. Scientists think it attacks fish by bending its body and then straightening out suddenly, the way a snake attacks, and swallowing the entire fish. Frilled shark teeth each have three points instead of one, which makes their bite even more effective.

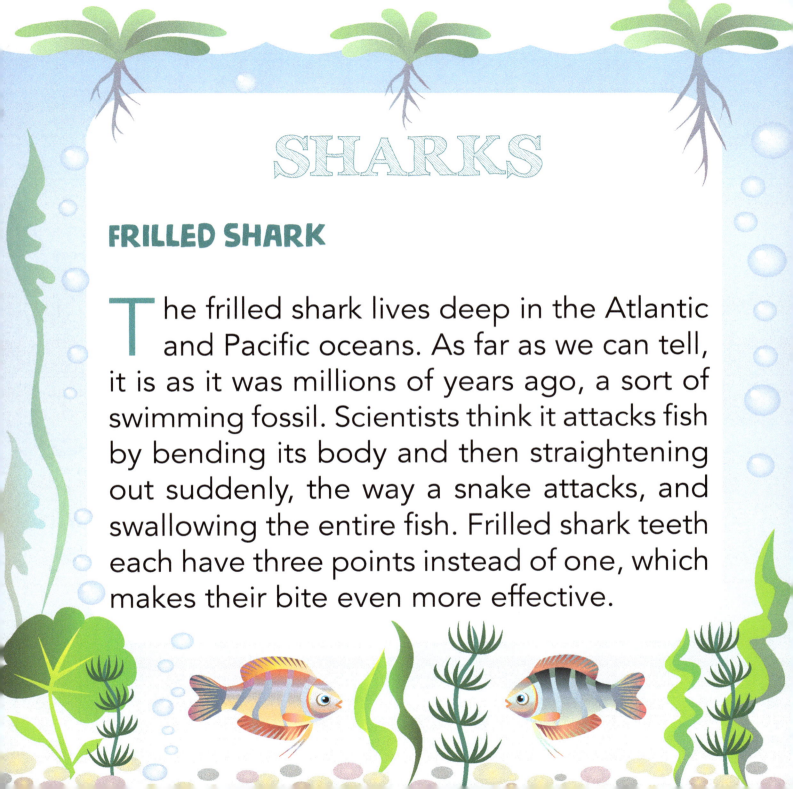

CHIMAERA

Chimaera are also known as "ghost sharks", partly because they are rarely seen. They used to live all through the oceans, but for various reasons now are only found in deep water.

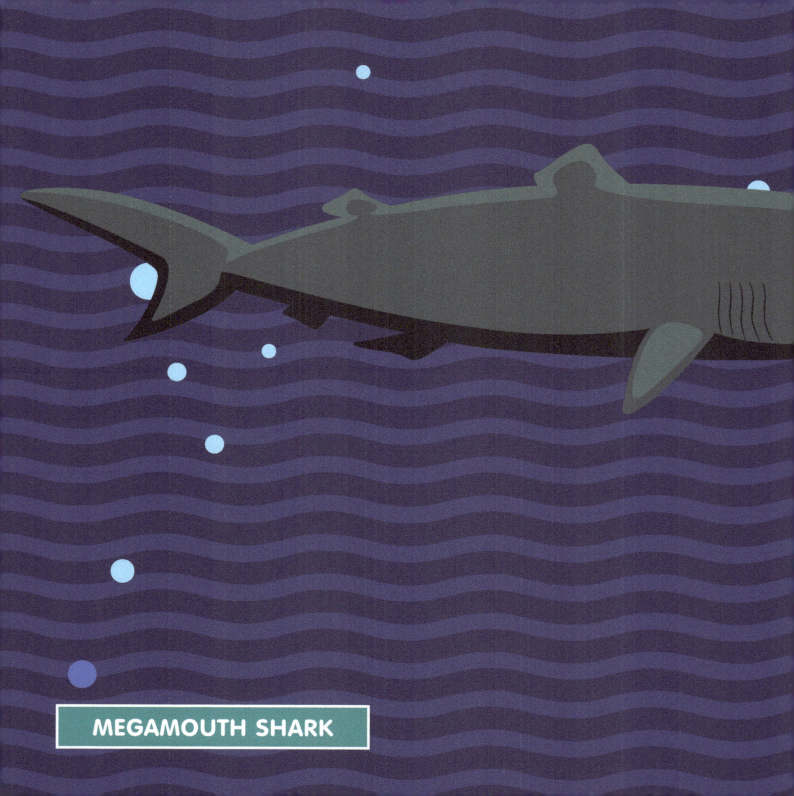

MEGAMOUTH SHARK

MEGAMOUTH SHARK

The first example of this deep-water shark was found in 1976! It is so new to us that scientists are still working on a classification for it. The shark probably opens its huge mouth very wide to collect many small fish or lots of plankton at a time. It also has a glowing light inside its mouth that attracts the fish it wants to eat!

The megamouth can grow to six meters long, yet we knew nothing about it until very recently. That shows how much we may still be missing in the deep ocean!

GOBLIN SHARK

We have only seen a few specimens of this scary-looking shark, brought up from the deeps in fishing nets. It has jaws it can extend and retract when dealing with things it wants to eat, but beyond that we know little of how it lives.

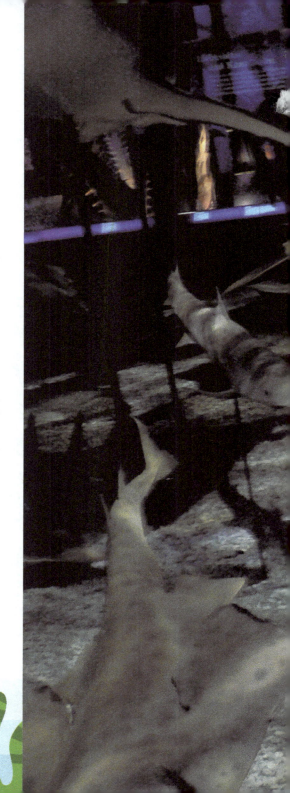

GOBLIN SHARK

BIG RED JELLYFISH

SOFT-BODIED CREATURES

BIG RED JELLYFISH

This jellyfish can be over one meter long. It doesn't have tentacles like many jellyfish; instead it has thick "feeding arms" that help it bring small fish to where the jellyfish can consume them.

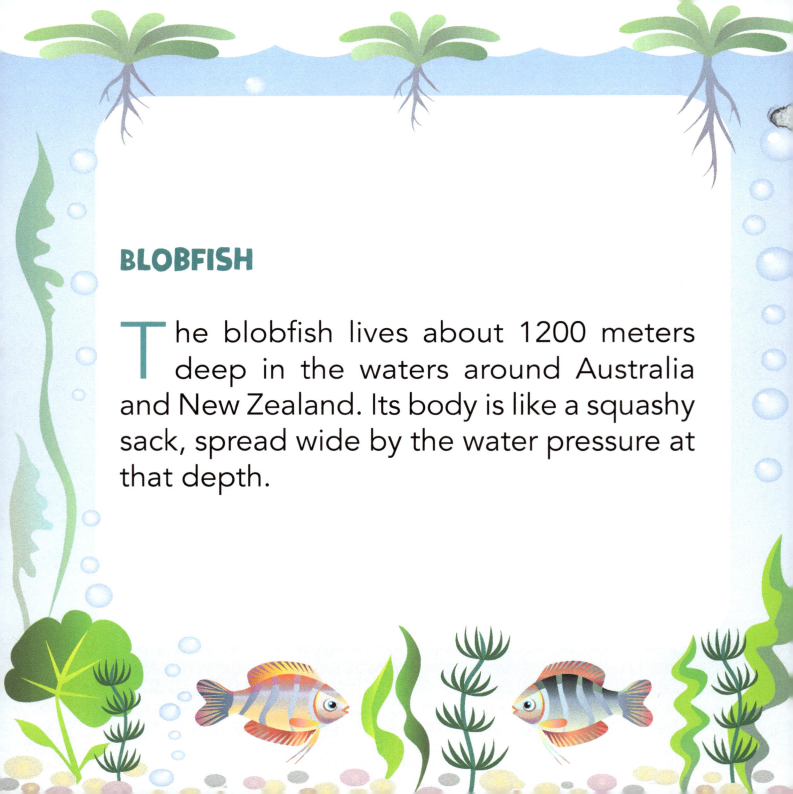

BLOBFISH

The blobfish lives about 1200 meters deep in the waters around Australia and New Zealand. Its body is like a squashy sack, spread wide by the water pressure at that depth.

OCTOPUS AND SQUID

VAMPIRE SQUID

The vampire squid has the largest eyes in proportion to its body of any animal on Earth that we know of. Although its red eyes and webbing like a cloak make it look like some sort of cartoon vampire, this squid does not actually suck blood.

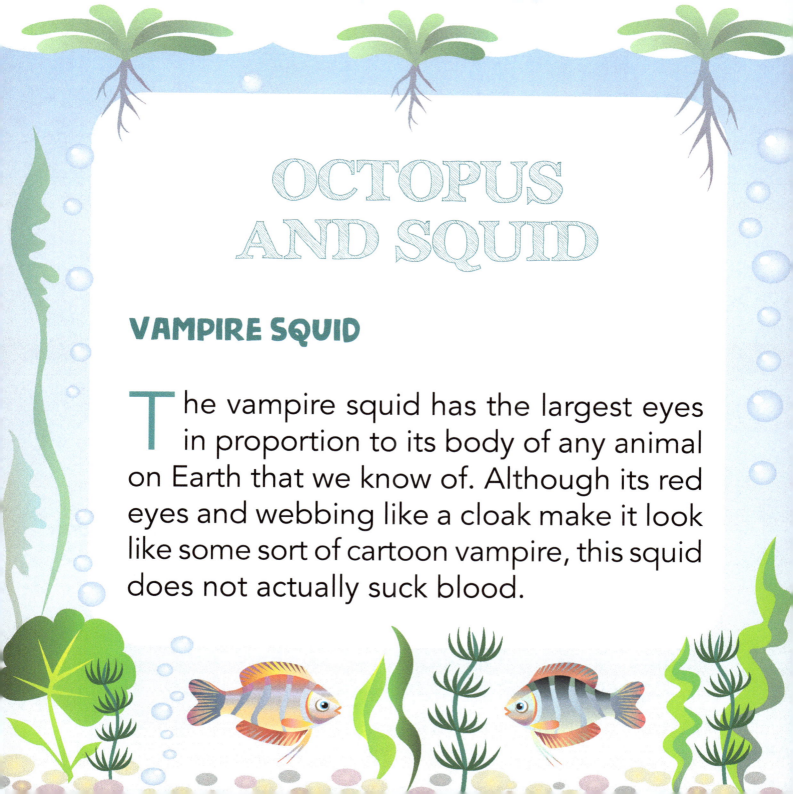

GIANT SQUID

These deep-water squid are so large that for a long time people thought they were imaginary, like giants in stories. Giant squid can grow to almost 20 meters long, as long as a six-story building is tall! Their eyes are as big as beach balls.

Giant squid are so big and capable that their only natural enemies are sperm whales. Sperm whales often show scars on their bodies that are marks of their battles with giant squid.

GIANT SQUID

BLUE RINGED OCTOPUS

This deep-sea creature may not look as scary as some others, but it is one of the most dangerous sea animals in existence. It uses a poisonous venom to kill its prey, and there is no known remedy for the poison.

OTHER CREATURES

GULPER EEL

This eel lives about 3,000 meters deep, and can be two meters long. We know very little about how gulper eels live, except for their feeding habits. They can enlarge their jaws so they can grab a fish that's as large as they are, and can expand their stomachs to hold their prey once they have swallowed it.

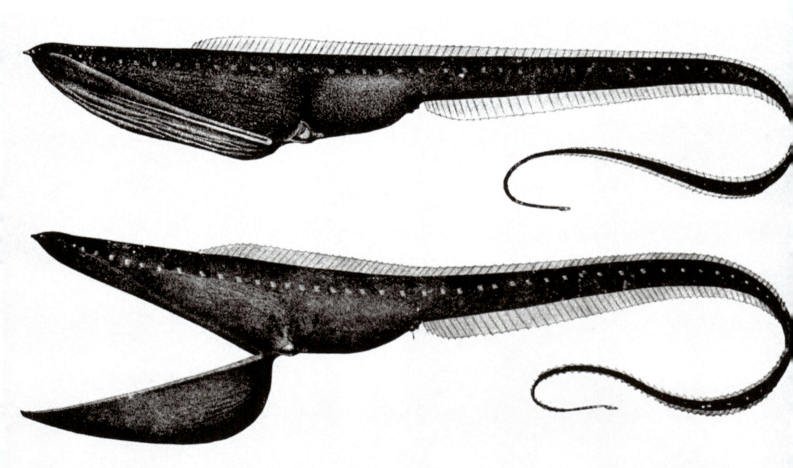

GIANT ISOPOD

GIANT ISOPOD

The isopod sticks to the bottom of the ocean in the north Atlantic and under the waters of the Arctic Circle. They can grow to about 30 centimeters long and mainly eat scraps of whatever they can find. However they sometimes attack other small creatures.

Isopods have been in the ocean for millions of years. Part of their survival skills is patience: they can go up to four years between meals!

AMPHIPOD

Amphipods are crustaceans, relatives to lobsters. They are normally quite small, and live deep at the bottom of the Pacific Ocean, but some specimens over a foot long have been captured.

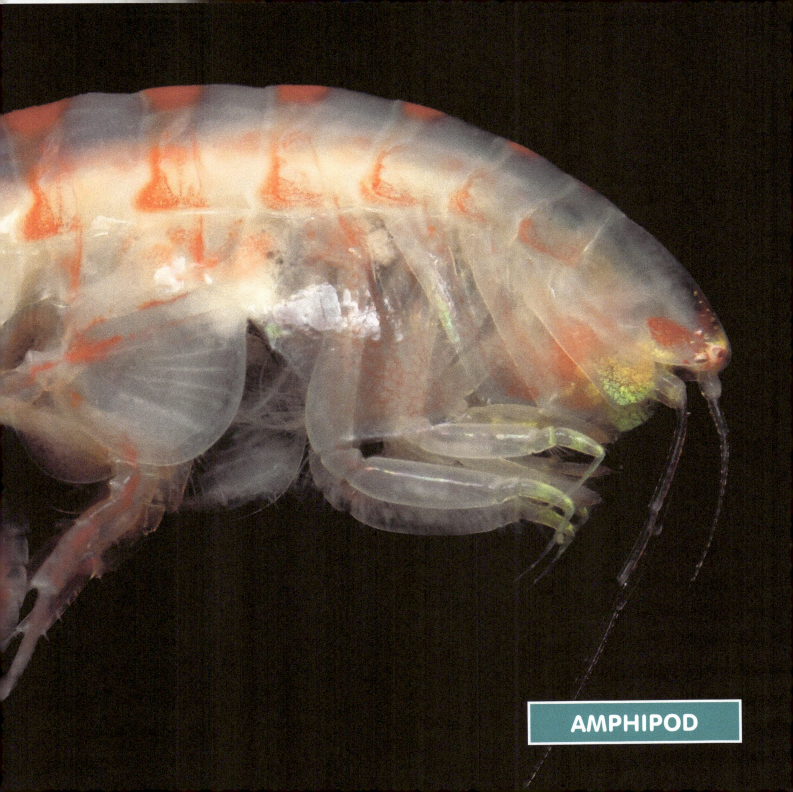

AMPHIPOD

GRENADIER

GRENADIER

Grenadiers are as much as fifteen percent of the population of the deep sea. They live as deep as six kilometers, where few other creatures can survive.

GIANT SPIDER CRAB

Giant spider crabs are the largest crabs on the planet, growing so large that they can be four meters from claw tip to claw tip! Fortunately for us, they live deep in the ocean: it would be hard to survive a bite from a claw like that!

GIANT SPIDER CRAB

TERRIBLE-CLAW LOBSTER

TERRIBLE-CLAW LOBSTER

These lobsters have claws of two different sizes, but we know so little about them that we are not sure why. The first examples of terrible-claw lobsters were only discovered, deep in the Pacific Ocean near the Philippines, in 2007.

LOTS MORE IN THE SEA!

We know far more about what lives on dry land than we do about what's in the sea. In fact, we may know as much about the surface of the Moon as we do about the bottom of the deepest ocean trenches. Learn more about what you might find in the sea in Baby Professor books like The Great White Shark, Penguins like Warm Water, Too!, and Ocean Tides and Tsunamis.

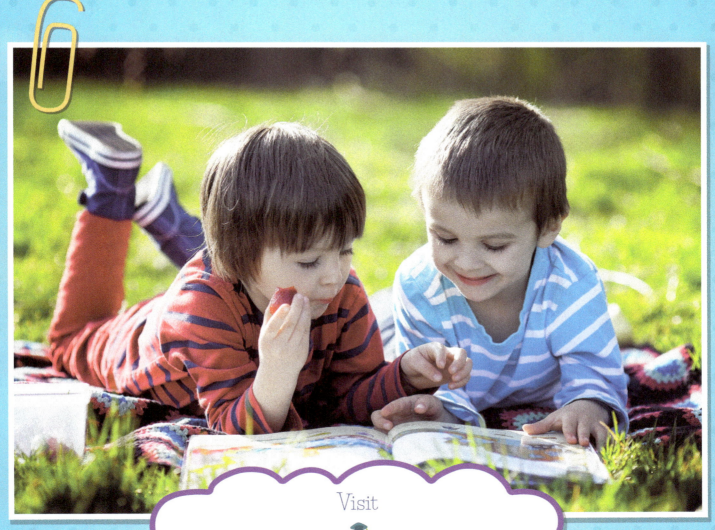

Visit

BABY PROFESSOR
EDUCATION KIDS

www.BabyProfessorBooks.com

to download Free Baby Professor eBooks
and view our catalog of new and exciting
Children's Books

Milton Keynes UK
Ingram Content Group UK Ltd.
UKHW050116050924
447642UK00021BA/35